ALWAYS BE THE LIGHT

WRITTEN BY
DEVEN TELLIS, ED.D

ILLUSTRATED BY
COURTNEY MONDAY

Manufactured in the United States of America

ISBN: 978-1-7374632-2-1

FIRST EDITION –

Illustrations: Courtney Monday

Editing: WesCourt Advisors

USA $14.99

DEDICATION:

To my kiddos,
With all my love...

There's no need to dim your LIGHT for anyone.

ACKNOWLEDGEMENTS:

A very special thanks is in order for my parents,
Ralph & Debora, for supporting my vision for
my book projects, believing in it, and always
doing whatever they can to help me to succeed.
They are the best, bar none.

Always be the light...
for you are precious

in *HIS SIGHT.*

If you're the only one, that's fine, just stand up tall and let it **SHINE.**

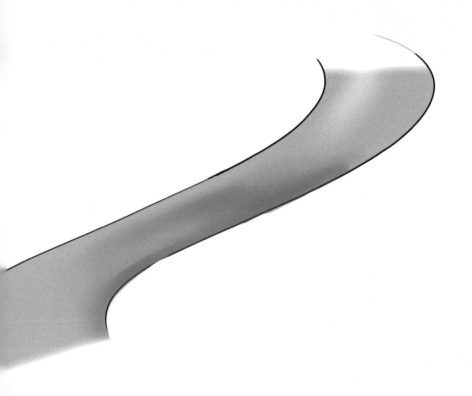

I'll always
always be the light...
for I have the

8

POWER
to invite...

with a special hug or helping hand,
a smile so wide, so warm and grand.

Forever be the gleaming light...
RESIST the wrong.

EMBRACE what's right.

Set the standard, break the mold, inspire others to be **BOLD.**

I'll be the everlasting light…
as I teach others

to *UNITE.*

Up with faith and down with fear.

In all our blessings, keep **HIM NEAR.**

Now and ever, be the light...
a twinkling

STAR,

a brilliant sight.

Beneath His glimmer from afar, there's no question *whose* you are!

I'll be the never-fading light...
and urge others

to take **FLIGHT.**

My arms reach out like wings unfurled, bringing **GREATNESS** to the world.

OTHER BOOKS BY THIS AUTHOR

Coming Soon

'Good News: We need more of it'

For More, Visit:
https://drdevencreates.com

CPSIA information can be obtained
at www.ICGtesting.com
Printed in the USA
BVHW022317310821
615693BV00003B/75